Pawsome Bark-Outs for *Saucy Aussie Living*

"I love this book. Read *Saucy Aussie Living* and get the second leash on life that you deserve!"
—**Brad Pitbull**

"I've had my ups and I've had my downs, and the best time to stay on top is when your second leash comes 'round."
—**Lady WoofWoof**

"A fool and his dog are soon parted. Luckily, the dog will find a better place, especially after reading *Saucy Aussie Living*."
—**Aristotle, canine philosopher**
(No relation to the other one.)

"Of all the strays I've caught, the ones who make the most of their second leashes are the ones who read *Saucy Aussie Living*."
—**Clint "The Dog Catcher" O'Maykish**

"Finally! A book about second leashes that makes sense."
—**Sparky Wigglebottom**

"I knew Ruby Red when she was on her first leash. Believe me, she knows what she's barking about!"
—**Mr. Blue, author of *True Blue Leadership* and *From Underdog to Wonder Dog***

"Cats don't wear leashes, but this book made even *me* want to get a second one!"
—**Allistair, the "International Cat of Mystery"**

www.TremendousLifeBooks.com

SAUCY AUSSIE LIVING

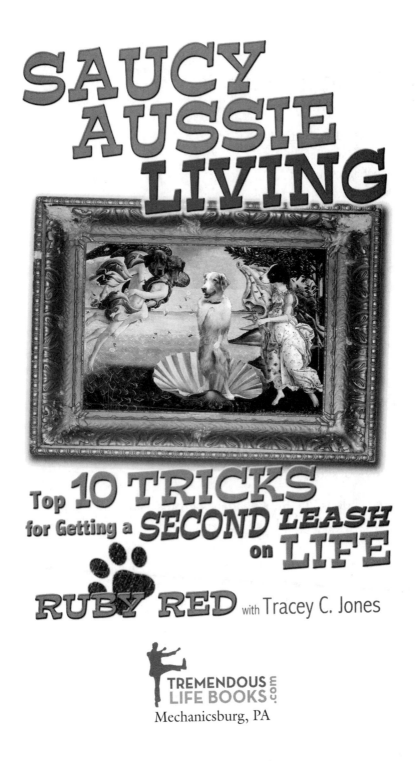

Top 10 TRICKS
for Getting a SECOND LEASH on LIFE

RUBY RED with Tracey C. Jones

TREMENDOUS
LIFE BOOKS.com

Mechanicsburg, PA

Tremendous Life Books
118 West Allen Street
Mechanicsburg, PA 17055
www.TremendousLifeBooks.com
www.facebook.com/TremendousLifeBooks
www.twitter.com/TraceyCJones

Front cover illustration by Mark Armstrong
Ruby Red Family Gallery illustrations by Neil McMillan
Design and layout by Anthony R. Michalski

ISBN-13 978-1-936354-29-0

Contents

Dedication

There's not a creature on this planet that doesn't need a second chance at some time in life. This book is dedicated to everyone who is living in a state of complete chaos and needs a new leash on life. It's also dedicated to all of the tremendous rescue groups whose mission is giving animals a second chance. They spend their limited resources working tirelessly to provide a means for doomed dogs to make the trek across borders and into the care of no-kill rescue shelters and selfless foster homes.

Many dogs who once had *furever* homes find themselves abandoned by their owners. Like so much in life, nothing comes with a guarantee; not a job, not a family, not even a home. Some of these creatures had owners who simply could not continue to support them, some had been trapped in abusive situations, and some were simply determined to have "outlived" their usefulness and were cast by the wayside.

Such was the case with Ruby Red. A magnificent, purebred, red merle Australian Shepherd, Ruby had produced numerous litters until the ripe old age of six when her owners decided she was of no more use to them and turned her over to a shelter. Ruby was scared. She hadn't been socialized, and she was deemed aggressive and sentenced to be euthanized. That's where a tremendous rescue organization came into play. Located in Carlisle, Pennsylvania, the founder made the trek to Bowling Green, Kentucky, to rescue Ruby. They took one look at her and realized that all she needed was a second leash on life. I am *furever* grateful that they did.

Ruby shared a lot of issues that many of us face when something dramatic has changed and we are left to deal with living life on completely new terms. Maybe it's an unexpected divorce or a pink slip at work; maybe it's realizing each day that you're unfulfilled and you're getting closer to the end of your leash. Ruby was in her mid-forties, in human years, and had been bare-pawed and pregnant her entire life! Now this middle-aged beauty queen found herself cast aside; no home, no skills, and no future.

I could relate, certainly not as a beauty queen, but because I too had suffered the painful fallout of people who had used me for what they could and then cast me aside. I bet that she could find her way in life again and took a chance. After countless commands, treats, heart-to–hearts, and belly rubs, Ruby gained her second leash on life. Today, she is so well adapted that she serves alongside her brother, Mr. Blue, the Chief Motivational Hound at Tremendous Life Books and best-smelling *pawthor* of *True Blue Leadership: Top 10 Tricks from the Chief Motivational Hound*. People say they cannot believe this is the same dog they saw when she first came home with me, and neither can I.

Watching Ruby Red's complete transformation reinforced many important life lessons for me. I never ceased to be amazed by the intelligence, ability to adapt to change, and thankfulness embodied in this creature. Her struggles reminded me of how I dealt with some of life's biggest upsets. It became obvious to me early on that if I mirrored more of Ruby Red's approach to change, I could catch all of the curveballs life threw at us.

So if you are faced with complete chaos in everything you've ever known and are too scared to know which way to turn just to chase your own tail, read on. It's impossible to live a life free from pain, but there are some ways to take the hurt and have it make you better rather than bitter. Ruby wanted me to share with you her Top Ten Tricks for Getting a Second Leash on Life. Obey these commands and discover the Saucy Aussie in you!

Acknowledgments

This book is dedicated to my soul dog, Mr. Blue, who allowed me to bring a second dog into the house after ten years of being an only canine kid. Your calm temperament and open heart allowed Ruby Red to find her *furever* home. I knew with you as her big brother she'd turn out perfect. I am humbled to have you by my side each and every day.

Thank you to woMAN's best friend, the dog, for being an endless source of *pawsitive* inspiration, to the amazing rescue groups that work to save what others cast away, and to the team at Tremendous Life Books. Your input and support is what makes me so tired of being happy, it's wearing me out. You are the greatest pack I've ever had the pleasure of working with. Thanks for being such amazing aunts and uncles to my fur pack and for loving them like they were your own.

Thanks to the reader for helping change the world one book—and one bark—at a time. May this book fully unleash the Saucy Aussie in you!

Foreword

On January 1, 2011, I adopted Ruby, a beautiful six-year-old red merle Aussie from Kentucky whose entire life had been spent having a succession of litters. That's all I knew about her. When the car pulled into my driveway with her in the back seat, she looked over at me and it was love at first sight. I may not be the best at picking relationships or jobs, but boy do I know my soul dogs when I see them.

I put a leash on her to take her for a trot around her new surroundings and to introduce her to Mr. Blue, her new brother, and her three new cat siblings. Like humans, my hound had some issues with taking it all in. They say that dogs exhibit aggression due to fear or dominance issues. Sounds like the two biggest problems that plague mankind as well!

The next few months were spent with behavioral specialists, reading numerous articles on the web, trying out various harnesses and muzzles, and in countless training and physical exercise sessions. Ruby's coat was greasy and at the same time brittle like straw. She had just been spayed and her sutures had come open and were bleeding. She had terrible digestive problems due to the stress and change in diet. My beauty queen was a mess! But I kept focused on those gorgeous almond eyes and saw her inner beauty. After all, she just didn't know that she was about to get a second leash on life. Would she be ready to accept this scary change for rewards she could not know existed? Are any of us?

Ruby cried incessantly whenever I left her sight. Every step I took she was right there behind me. She barked at anything and everything. I thought about naming her Ethel Merman, the loudest, brassiest redhead I had ever seen. She was dominant and demanded nonstop attention. She had not been trained to behave while leashed and walks were like trying to hold on to a bucking bronco. She didn't know how to jump into the Jeep or even catch a Frisbee! Imagine that! An agility-loving dog who didn't know how to catch a Frisbee!

All the while, I'm watching her struggle unnecessarily when I know that the whole world is open to her. When she discovers this and learns to relax and to walk calmly beside me, we'll enjoy a lifetime of exploring all of the wonders, sights, and smells the world has to offer. And I will be there to protect, nourish, and love her unconditionally *furever*. They say getting a second leash is when you realize it's all about how you respond, not react, to the things in your life. And as the months passed, that's exactly the realization that Ruby came to as well.

Today, Ruby Red is the Chief Excitement Officer (CEO) at Tremendous Life Books, where we work together every day changing the world one book, and one bark, at a time! My father, and Ruby Red's *grandpaw*, was Charlie "Tremendous" Jones, a renowned public speaker who addressed hundreds of thousands of people through a career that spanned over fifty years. He used to say, "You're the same today as you'll be in five years except for two things: the people you meet and the books you read." This book is a product of that philosophy.

So now I'll turn you over to Ruby Red. She's learned some amazing things in her first year with us. Let her share what she's discovered.

May this book inspire you, Saucy Aussie, that all things happen to make us better, not bitter!

Ruby Red's Bark-tion-ary

In this book, Ruby Red uses some words that are unique to the canine tongue. Here are those words and their human translation.

bark-out	=	shout-out
barkful	=	thankful
furever	=	forever
grandpaw	=	grandpa
pawsitive	=	positive
pawsome	=	awesome
pawthor	=	author
ruff	=	rough
ruff said	=	enough said

SAUCY AUSSIE LIVING

Get the "H" Out of Here!

1

How to Turn a Threat into a Treat

We've all heard the phrase, "Let's get the 'h' out of here," where the "h" stands for "h-e-double toothpicks": Hades, Lucifer's lair, Hell! But I'd like to point out a more *pawsitive* meaning to this oft-used phrase.

When I was adopted into my *furever* home, everything was *new* to me; and *new* meant *scary* because it was a change from what I was used to. Many humans and hounds alike view change as a threat, even when it's meant to be a *pawsitive* change. If I could have spoken human words to my new mom, I wouldn't even have been able to express myself! Fear frothed freely from my jowls. I just couldn't take it all in! Everything scared me and I reacted negatively to the leash, to people, to other dogs, to cars, you name it! It all freaked me out and I let my mom know it.

> **"Consider how hard it is to change yourself and you'll understand what little chance you have in trying to change others."**
> **—Jacob M. Braude**

So my mom hired a behavioral specialist, a type of dog whisperer, if you will. I thought to myself, "Good luck getting me to hear your whispers over my anxious, repetitive barking and growling!" However, this woman was tremendous.

"Stressed spelled backward is desserts!"

It's like she could read my mind. She immediately recognized that I was a quick learner with a strong desire to please. She told my mom that with those two traits alone, everything would be just fine.

What? Was she talking about *me*?

I could feel a little of the anxiety begin to drain off as I realized these people were talking about me in a *pawsitive* manner! Do you know what that means to a human or a hound when they are given *pawsitive* reinforcement? It's one of the greatest motivators you can bestow upon another living being. So the first point I must make is that knowledge *really is king*, and if it doesn't kill you, *it truly does* make you stronger. The more you know and experience, the less you fear. So if you are *willing* to learn a few new tricks you can begin turning threats into treats!

With each new sight or sound, my mom looked into my eyes, spoke calmly, and plied me with treats. Slowly I began to realize that things that had previously scared me were now harbingers of hamburger! (More like turkey hotdogs and tuna casserole brownies, but they were good too!) I quickly learned how to turn a "threat" into a "treat" by getting the "h" out of there. One little change in your attitude leads to a whole different outlook on life. You just have to

"Adopting the right attitude can convert a negative stress into a positive one."
— Hans Selye

Get the "H" Out of Here!

"He who rejects change is the architect of decay. The only human institution which rejects progress is the cemetery."
—Harold Wilson

be open to it!

There are countless stories of humans who have lost everything only to discover what it was that they really wanted to begin with. Sometimes we hold what we have so tightly in our grasp that we can't open our paws and hands to receive the new leash that life is waiting to hand us.

A pink slip can be the catalyst to move you into another professional field or even to start your own business.

A divorce can be the chance to find happiness within yourself or with someone who treats you the way you deserve to be treated.

Not getting a certain promotion just means there's something else better waiting in store for you that is a much, much, much better fit.

In my previous life I would never have willingly walked out of my breeding cage. But had I known then what my new life held in store I would have jumped the fence long ago! You just have to have the courage to accept and even seek change and look at life's setbacks as stepping-stones to a greater life. And when you're faced with rejection, take time for reflection. As the late, great Winston Churchill said so eloquently, "Success is going from failure to failure with no loss of enthusiasm."

My mom often jokes that she thanks God that she never got the things she thought she really wanted. There were several times when she had to restart everything and find a new job and a new home. People she thought would be in her life forever suddenly abandoned or betrayed her. It was *ruff*, but she

"Do one thing every day that frightens you."
—Eleanor Roosevelt

knew there was a plan for it all, even if she couldn't see it at the time. She believed with all her heart that something better was always right beyond her line of sight and she lived her life based on this principle. And something better always *did* come to pass because when you develop the right perspective, *you* define the better outcome that awaits you.

How exciting is *that*, Saucy Aussie?

Her endless cycle of successes and setbacks are the very things that led her right to where she was meant to be to-day. There's a much bigger plan operating for all humans and second-chance hounds. All we have to do is be willing to re-spond, not react, and to willingly accept change in a *pawsitive* manner. A closed doggie door just means that there is a much greater one ready to be charged through right around the cor-ner! Change is good! It's meant to develop us into everything we were meant to be. So, Saucy Aussie, reverse any curse by realizing that threats are just treats in disguise.

Here's a little exercise for you. When my mom was in the military, she said they used a lot of acronyms. So I came up with one of my own. When something *cat*astrophic (figures there'd be a cat at the root!) or even unsettling happens in your life, think FIDO: **Forget It and Drive On!** Tom Cochrane was right: life is a highway and I want to ride it all night long—with my head hanging out the window. The scenery on the road of life is *furever* chang-ing. The only time it doesn't is when you're about to get hit from behind. So move it!

To those of you who say, "I'm an old dog and I can't or won't learn new tricks," I say, "Talk to the paw!" No-

"Progress is impossible without change, and those who cannot change their minds cannot change anything."
—George Bernard Shaw

body wants to go through life full of fear and aggression no matter how gray in the muzzle they are. It takes years off your life and we dogs don't have a long enough lifespan as it is! Are you teaching your pups at home or your pack at work how to turn being stressed into desserts? Knowledge and repetition are the keys. They say it takes forty days to internalize a habit, and I'd have to say that's about when I started feeling like my bark was worse than my bite. And don't get your fur ruffled if it takes time or if you suffer a setback. All it takes is a commitment to continuous learning and every Saucy Aussie reading this book has that. So live life with zest, not fear, and let's all get the "h" out of here!

Here's to embracing change and unleashing the Saucy Aussie in you!

Extra Sauce!

*Who Moved My Cheese? An A-Mazing Way to Deal
With Change in Your Work and in Your Life*
by Spencer Johnson, M.D.

This is one of the simplest, yet most powerful, metaphors on change ever written. They call it a gem because it is small and incredibly valuable, and that's exactly what this book is. From one of the most recognized experts on management comes a charming parable filled with insights designed to help readers manage change quickly and prevail in changing times.

Who Moved My Cheese? is a simple parable that reveals profound truths about change. It is an amusing and enlightening story of four characters who live in a "maze" and look for "cheese" to nourish them and make them happy. "Cheese" is a metaphor for what you want to have in life—whether it is a good job, a loving relationship, money, a possession, health, or spiritual peace of mind. "The maze" is where you look for what you want—the organization you work in or the family or community you live in.

The characters are faced with unexpected change. Eventually, one of them deals with it successfully and writes what he has learned from his experience on the maze walls. When you come to see "the handwriting on the wall," you can discover for yourself how to deal with change so that you can enjoy less stress and more success (however you define it) in your work and in your life.

This book has many valuable lessons to teach every Saucy Aussie how to turn any threat into a treat and gain a second leash on life!

Bark Through That Muzzle

2

She Who Barks Last, Barks Best!

When my mom first brought me home I barked non-stop. I just couldn't keep quiet! I had a reaction to everything. Sometimes it was out of curiosity, joy, fear, and sometimes it was just to test the limits of who was boss. After all, I'm an Aussie, and barking is just part of our genetic coding. But then I learned that there is an art and a science to knowing when to be quiet and knowing when to bark, even if you've been muzzled. Did you know that there are times you should not be quiet, even when someone tries to silence you? They key is to know if and when you are barking up the wrong tree and should be quiet, or if you should continue to voice your concerns.

"If things go wrong, don't go with them."
—Roger Babson

You humans have something similar to this predicament. You call them *whistle blowers*: someone who reports dishonest or illegal activities occurring in a government department, a public or private organization, or a company. Chances are, these people tried to bring these issues to the attention of their own bosses and were told to put a muzzle on it!

How unfortunate that when someone alerts a supervisor, parent, teacher, preacher or politician that something is wrong, they are told to be quiet or the supervisor pretends he doesn't see it or ignores the fact that it's his responsibility to resolve it. Don't you know that the truth will set you free while covering up a wrongdoing may land you in an even bigger doghouse? This fear is still not big enough to stop some bad dogs from being a part of this huge problem.

No one can make you do anything that is illegal, immoral, or unethical. So before you use the excuse that everybody's doing it or you don't want to rock the boat, remember: Sometimes you are going to have to do the right thing and jump off that ship *before* it sinks. Floating in the sea of ethics can often be a lonely place. All around you are people who sat beside you during the annual HR and ethics training year after year, but don't want to hear about any problems. Why is that? George MacDonald said, "To be trusted is a greater compliment than to be loved." Yes, everyone is so obsessed with being liked that they often forget this critical point.

The reason people ignore doing the "right" thing is because *compliance* is not the same as *commitment*. There's a real difference between following the letter of the law and actually doing the right thing. Many want people to "like" them so they don't rock the boat or stop detrimental behavior even when they are well aware it's going on. People who are *committed* to some-

> **"The world is a dangerous place, not because of those who do evil, but because of those who look on and do nothing."**
> **—Albert Einstein**

thing do the right thing no matter who is watching because it's in their character to do so. People who simply *comply* do so out of fear for their reputation or to stay out of trouble. Those who are *committed* do what is right, regardless of the fallout, simply because it's the right thing to do.

We've all seen the devastating results of situational ethics in corporations and religious institutions; humans get to the top and forget all about their standards and morals. My mom recently read a Harvard Business Study that said that severe ethical or criminal lapses at the top were caused by the individuals forgetting the very things that got them there. Forgetting? We've seen horrendous falls from grace, even in the Bible. How can you forget what you've sworn to uphold? You don't forget it; you chose to silence it or ignore it because it was in your head and not in your heart. Or you convinced yourself that you were committed to something when you never actually were. It's a classic case of head knowledge versus heart knowledge. You don't *forget* what you carry in your heart.

Our standard of Saucy Aussie living is the *gold* standard: It is constant. As top dogs, we see things in black and white, literally, and not in shades of gray. You cannot be one way at home and one way at work or church; one way to your boss and one way to your people. That's wrong. When you are one way at one time and another way at another time, you'll get a reputation for barking out of both sides of your mouth! Have you heard the one about the boss who pulls into the corporate parking lot at 8am on Monday, bows his head and prays, "Lord, I'll be back in touch Friday after 5pm"?

"It is easy to dodge our responsibilities, but we cannot dodge the consequences of dodging our responsibilities."
—Sir Josiah Stamp

It's critical to live life authentically and in congruence with the agreements that we've sworn to uphold. Our public and our private personas must be in sync. Actions are a manifestation of conscience. Are you a jerk at work while saving your best for all the rest? Or does your pack at home want to flush you down the commode when you enter your abode. Are you yelling in your dwelling or are you a mouse in the house? As Charlie "Tremendous" Jones said, "One of life's greatest challenges is how to quit *acting* and start *being*."

No amount of pressure can excuse you from being a Saucy Aussie who is true to your conscience. When we get squeezed, whatever is in us will come out. Humans love to justify their wishy-washiness saying, "Oh, the fame, the power, the money blinded me." Talk to the paw! You weren't blinded; what was already inside you came out. Abraham Lincoln said, "Nearly all men can stand adversity, but if you want to test a man's character, give him power."

My mom personally experienced a different moral code of conduct when she attended the Air Force Academy in Colorado Springs, Colorado. The Acadey motto is inscribed on the Honor Wall: "We will not lie, steal, or cheat, nor tolerate among us anyone who does." Violations of this code could lead to expulsion. We all have moral codes we have promised to follow and uphold. It could be a nondisclosure agreement, a marital vow, or a non-compete. By signing on with an employer you are also bound by their human resources stan-

"History will have to record that the greatest tragedy of this period of social transition was not the strident clamor of the bad people, but the appalling silence of the good people."
—Martin Luther King Jr.

dards, which are often printed in a policy manual. If you cannot abide by these rules and commit them to heart, and not just your head, you need to take a long drink from the water bowl of reality. And if you try to muzzle someone enforcing the standards, bad dog! You should run for the hills with your tail between your legs. You have no business trying to hang with a pack of Saucy Aussies.

Be a Better Barker

There's No Such Thing as "Business" Ethics
by John C. Maxwell

Enron, Tyco, WorldCom, the Catholic Church, the housing bubble. You think no one saw these issues coming? Wrong. Someone knew and chose to stay muzzled, and others tried to bark out a warning and were quickly silenced by higher-ups or outside watchdog agencies that were corrupt, complicit, or weak.

Mr. Maxwell talks about the golden rule and why it's golden. He then goes on to discuss the five factors that can tarnish it: pressure, pleasure, power, pride, and priorities. These are the very things that every Saucy Aussie has to deal with, so it's essential to know when to bark through that muzzle if someone is trying to silence you.

Barking at the right time is all about knowing what's inside of you. You must be resolute in your knowledge and conviction of what is acceptable behavior and what might present danger. You and only you are responsible for your actions. If someone tries to silence you for doing the right thing, you need to bark up a different tree until you find someone who will notice. Being tolerant of wrongdoing is just as bad as doing it yourself. Know in your heart what you're barking about and anyone who tries to muzzle you can "talk to the paw!"

Every Saucy Aussie knows that she who barks last, barks best!

Peace, Love, and Belly Rubs

3

Nothing Is So Bad It Can't Be Fixed with a Belly Rub

They say the way to a man's heart is through his stomach. So it is with dogs, our bellies in particular, and how we melt when our humans take the time to rub them. (We also, like men, fall deeply in love with treat dispensers.) People use the term "belly up" to describe something that has failed and died. It can also refer to a business or personal relationship that has fizzled out and is no longer viable. But in the canine world, belly up means just the opposite of all the negative human connotations. It signifies something pretty tremendous: a belly rub!

But bellies were not always such a pleasant experience for me. You see, I was living in the proverbial belly of the beast, smack-dab in the middle of a very bad situation, confined as a breeding dog, which for canines is like being in the central command of the enemy's headquarters. We need freedom and space, not imprisonment, squeezing out litter after litter. I felt trapped in this enclosed, unpleasant place, like the

Biblical story of Jonah who was swallowed by the great fish and spent three days entombed inside its belly.

"When you feel down at the mouth, think of Jonah. He came out all right."

— Anonymous

My mom was a little freaked out by me when we first met. I was wild on the leash, wild when I saw other dogs, wild when I saw other people, and wild whenever she was out of my sight. She went through the list of stressors with me to see what set me off and what calmed me. Although I was leash-aggressive, I wasn't food-aggressive. Strange people and animals upset me, but my own canine and feline siblings immediately became my best friends.

One thing my mom noticed is that I would immediately roll over on my belly for her to give me a tummy scratch. She instinctively knew that no matter how aggressive I was in other situations, if I would roll over and offer up my belly, I really was capable of being submissive. I just didn't know how to communicate with or react to those other hounds, humans, and events. But if rubbing my tummy could soothe this savage beast, she knew she had a starting point. The other thing my mom saw is that I allowed myself to be vulnerable. And that's sometimes tough for us Saucy Aussie types, to allow ourselves as bosses, or parents, or spouses to be completely vulnerable to another individual. We're used to being in control, large, and in charge, the last bark. You don't always need to be Snarky McBarky; move on over to *Chillville* and see how the other half lives.

"Scratch a dog and you'll find a permanent job."

—Franklin P. Jones

It's critical to do some self-examination; namely, what brings out the *beast* in you? It's so funny that humans call them pet peeves. We pets couldn't agree more! Did you know that the word *peevish* means ornery or ill-tempered? That perfectly describes

"There is no psychiatrist in the world like a puppy licking your face."
—Bern Williams

my first two months. You humans harbor your own set of annoyances that set you off as well! They are very idiosyncratic and personal. These are the things that bug you worse than a tick on the end of your tail. Maybe it's the doorbell; maybe it's sitting in a meeting, or people who state the obvious. Maybe it's drivers who don't use their turn signals, humans who snap their gum so loud it sounds like a BB gun, double-dipping chip grazers, leaving the toilet seat up, letting cell phones ring in church, not clearing the remaining time on the microwave after the food is cooked, or drinking coffee out of a clear mug that makes you go "grrrrrrrrrrrrr."

Have you ever felt like biting off someone's head before they even open their mouth? We've all had days like that; sometimes even weeks or months! But once you talk to them and hear what they have to say, you sure feel great that you didn't! There's a great Chinese proverb that I always remember: **If you are patient in one moment of anger, you will escape a hundred days of sorrow.** So find that *something* that keeps you happy in your thoughts and words, and let it keep you from jumping to the end of your leash.

So what's the one thing or person that brings out the best in you and allows you to be at ease and connect with someone? Some say its music because music soothes the savage beast. My *grandpaw*, Charlie "Tremendous" Jones, spoke about the healing power of music and laughter. The dog whisperer knew she had to speak to me in my language. And that's exactly what she did. What's the one buzzword, tone, event, tail wag, association, link, or bond that turns you from snarky dog to happy dog? For me, like so many other hounds, it was a no-brainer: a belly rub.

Take time to identify what brings you inner peace amidst the sea of turmoil, even when you're in the belly of the whale. Is it something as simple as a smile? A cup of morning java that takes the edge off of the day? Chocolate? A long, hot, soaking bath? A nap? A long walk? A talk with a dear friend? A hand-written letter? A kind word? Medication? Prayer? A shoulder to cry on? For my mom it was talking with her father. When we deal with people, a lot of times we have our hackles up. They are buggin' us, baby! So stop and take time to find some common ground. Maybe compliment them on something they're wearing. Take time to ask them where they are from or if they have children. Once you find that common sweet spot, it's all good. Instead of people and situations bringing out the beast in you, they bring out the *best* in you.

Folklore says that rubbing Buddha's potbelly brings good fortune and wealth. But he's more than just a good-luck charm favored by Chinese restaurateurs and businessmen. The laughing Buddha's big belly is a symbol of tolerance and that prosperity and wealth can go hand-in-hand with enlightened awareness. So don't be so *Ruddha*; be happy like Buddha! Once you find your inner belly rub, you'll exude peace and happiness and be able to tolerate the things that get under your fur. Peace, love, and belly rubs *furever*!

Bark and Sell!

The Art of Persuasion

by Bob Burg

The Art of Persuasion teaches you how to get what you want when you want it. Every Saucy Aussie would love to have that ability, right? *Ruff said.*

After studying some of the most successful men and women in modern history, author Bob Burg noticed how many common characteristics these people have and he shares them all with you.

One trait that stands above all the rest is their ability to win people over to their way of thinking; they were all persuasive. Each of these life winners had a burning desire, coupled with great creativity and a total, unshakable belief in their mission or cause.

Winning principles you will learn include:

- Making People Feel Important
- Everything Is Negotiable
- Dealing with Difficult People
- Persuasion in Action
- What Sets You Apart from the Rest
- Nuggets of Wisdom

Presented in everyday, clear, and often humorous language, *The Art of Persuasion* leaves an impression on you that will last a lifetime—one filled with one success after another! You'll be able to deliver a proverbial belly rub in any situation, no matter how difficult, aimed at getting what you want through persuasion and not intimidation.

"I am still determined to be cheerful
and happy, in whatever situation I may
be; for I have also learned from
experience that the greater part of
our happiness or misery depends
upon our dispositions and not upon
our circumstance."
                    —Martha Washington

Don't Be a Bulldog in a China Shop

4

Dog-ling Rivalry Bites!

When I first arrived at my new home I was beside myself. I now had a large, beautiful home with an adoring new mom and three cat siblings. Even though I'm a herding dog, I was very gentle with the felines in the house. I had given birth to numerous litters, so taking care of these smallish creatures reminded me of all my pups! I cleaned their ears and ran my teeth up and down their coat to get the "nits" off. I was right at home. But I also had another sibling, my canine brother, Mr. Blue. He and my mom had been together as a pack since he was five weeks old. What a lucky dog! We took it slow the first two days as I struggled to figure out where I fit in.

On day three, however, things came to a head and the fur and fangs were flying as Mr. Blue and I locked muzzles. Luckily, the activity was mostly symbolic and we quickly calmed back down. I am more excitable and vocal, but Mr. Blue is the alpha in the house. That was that; case closed. My mom is very affectionate with all of her fur-children, taking care to spend special time with each of us while brushing, petting, hugging, and telling the timeless tale of how each and every one of us came into her life. But this intense camaraderie and one-on-one was all new to me. No human had ever uttered sweet nothings into my ear, and I liked it so much that I could not contain myself or express myself properly!

Every time my mom knelt down to spend time with Mr. Blue or one of my cat siblings, I pushed my way right in front of them. I would even step on top of the cats, causing them to make a quacking sound like a duck. I abruptly flicked my muzzle under my mom's hand to forcefully get her attention away from Mr. Blue. I wanted to be the center of her world 24/7! I guess I assumed that the first six years of my life, where I missed out on all of the ear scratching and belly rubbing, gave me the right to act like a bulldog in a china shop.

I was falling prey to *dog-ling* rivalry, the four-legged kin to the dreaded sibling rivalry. Sibling rivalry is as old as time. In fact, the very first recorded murder in the history of mankind is found in the Book of Genesis when Cain killed his younger brother, Abel. Talk about a dog-eat-dog world! Sibling rivalry has been a thorn in the side of mankind (and in the paw of *dogdom*) ever since. It's as difficult to deal with now as it was then. And it can manifest itself not just with blood relatives, but with business peers as well.

My advice to all you Saucy Aussies in the house who are getting your second leash on life is to relax and don't let your fur get ruffled by the dog treats that others may be getting. Don't blow a good thing by walking into a new job, home, or relationship and act

"Never let an angry sister comb your hair."
—Patricia McCann

like you are "owed" something! My *grandpaw* wrote about these types of people in his book *Life Is Tremendous*. When he was a life insurance salesman he would interview prospective agents. Some of them sat there as if they were checking out the potential job to see if it could give them what *they* deserved. My *grandpaw* stopped these entitlement babies right in their tracks just like my mom stopped *my* rude behavior. I finally realized there was more than enough love and *pawsitive* interaction in my new environment to go around and I did not have to try to demand it all for myself.

Remember, you only get one chance to make a *pawsitive* first impression, so take a deep pant and be gentle until the awkwardness subsides. Treat each interaction as if it's a new beginning. Wait your turn. Don't be jealous of how much attention others are getting. Your time for a pat on the head and the recognition you deserve will come soon enough. Don't try to upstage others when it's their turn to shine. Sit, like a good dog, until you are called.

It's hard to contain yourself and not be jealous when others get *pawsitive* reinforcement. Recognition is such a powerful thing and jealously is one of the darkest and most potent forces in the universe. Sibling rivalry is rooted in a perceived lack of resources, i.e., the love and recognition of the parents or, in the corporate setting, from the boss. But just remember that there are infinite amounts of it, so no need to be jealous. Don't compete at work for recognition, don't compete in your home for affection, and don't compete with your friends for attention.

> "A beginning is the time for taking the most delicate care...."
> —Frank Herbert, from *Dune*

A Saucy Aussie knows that *only* when you realize you have nothing to prove do you have everything to gain. So don't let the green-eyed monster ruin a good thing. There's plenty of love and opportunity in the world if you just wait your turn and don't get hot under the collar about what you perceive others are getting. Keep your mind open and be thankful for all the tremendous changes coming your way. Enjoy your second leash on life and count your many blessings on each of the claws on your paws!

From Pushy Pooch to Golden Retriever

How to Win Friends and Influence People
by Dale Carnegie

Dealing with people and pooches is the biggest problem every human and hound faces in life. This book is the definitive guide to successful interaction. They say that success in life, business, and just about anything else is 15 percent technical skill and 85 percent communications skill. So it's critical that you read this book so you can truly get a second leash on life.

Whether you're in sales, management, or running a household, you need to know how to win friends and influence people, no bones about it. Every Saucy Aussie has a desire to learn and a deep determination to get along with others in the pack. As long as you have these two things, this book will turn you into the top dog with whom everyone wants to associate!

Why, the very first chapter is called "If You Want to Gather Honey, Don't Kick Over the Beehive." That's exactly what I was doing when I first started my new life. I behaved like a bulldog in a china shop. This book will give you fundamental techniques in handling people, six ways to make people like you, how to win people to your way of thinking without having to step all over them, and how to be a Saucy Aussie leader without giving offense or arousing resentment.

This book is a *must read*. If no one taught you these time-tested principles of successful interaction, please take the time to read all about them and discover what they can do for you. This book has transformed countless Saucy Aussies from pushy pooches to golden retrievers of people's admiration and support. I told my mom that the principles in this book were the most instrumental things in changing my personality from dogmatic to *pawsome*!

"It's a dog-eat-dog world, Woody, and I'm wearing milk-bone underwear."
—Norm from *Cheers*

Which Side of the Fence Are You On?

5

If You Chase Two Rabbits, They Will Both Get Away

Australian shepherds are a breed known for their gorgeous multi-colored coats. They can even have a color marking on their head called "split-face." This describes a pattern where one side of the face is a solid color and the other has a merle pattern. There may be a white stripe in the center of our faces that further accentuates this striking feature. While being split-faced is a very beautiful thing in canine *dogdom*, being "two-faced" in man's kingdom most definitely is not. Some humans have the bad habit of talking out of both sides of their mouths when they "speak" and cannot make up their mind which side of the fence they're on.

In his classic speech, *The Price of Leadership*, my *grandpaw*, Charlie "Tremendous" Jones, asked, "What are you going to

**"There is no more miserable human being than one in whom nothing is habitual but indecision."
—William James**

live your life in, who are you going to live it with, and what are you going to live it for? Know that you're living for yourself or know that you're living it for God, but don't straddle the fence." It's important to remember that when you chase two rabbits, they both get away. So pick your pack, your career, and your goals; then mark them…over and over and over.

Many humans and hounds have dualities in their temperament, which is great. For example, my mom loves to romp with us but she has no problem being the disciplinarian when she needs to be. She's also a true extrovert but just loves a weekend where we do nothing but hang out at the house together. My brother, Mr. Blue, is part Australian Shepherd and part basset hound, so he gets as much enjoyment from leaping in the air to catch a Frisbee as he does dragging his nose along a scent on the ground.

The various facets of your personality add dimension and define your uniqueness. Humans and hounds also have the tremendous ability to change their minds as new information creates new convictions and patterns. For example, something we once tolerated we may now feel convicted about. Something we may have previously feared we can now embrace. Don't be afraid to evolve in your convictions and wisdom.

Why, look at me! I was once deemed so aggressive that I was pronounced un-adoptable! But when my mom unlocked my inner ability to be sweet, obedient, and calm, I experienced a whole new outlook on life. You can and will evolve as your convictions change and become stronger. You humans call it developing "good judgment," and now I can hardly keep my tail from shaking nonstop because I have so much of it! Gotta' love that *hound wisdom*!

"When you rationalize, you tell yourself rational lies."
—Ruby Red

Which Side of the Fence Are You On?

My *grandpaw* used to say, "I'm so tired of being happy, it's wearing me out!" And when you're acting true to your convictions, that's how you experience life.

Life's experiences have the ability to make us more empathetic if we use them wisely. The more we walk around the ring of life in another person's paws, the greater our ability to see things from their viewpoint. That's what makes the *pain* in growing pains worth it. But beware of over-rationalizing everything. If you stand for nothing you'll fall for anything. And when you *rationalize*, you tell yourself *rational lies*. Convictions are a tricky thing. Many of life's greatest challenges come the moment you decide whether to draw a line in the sand or step to the other side. Saucy Aussies know the rules and codes that guide their lives and they follow them with all their might.

I recently broke my code of obedience and told myself a rational lie. My mom often brings leftovers from home into the workplace to share with the pack. One day, she had a large plate of whoopie pies set on the conference room table. Now I know I'm not supposed to put my paws up on the table and help myself to treats, but on this day, since there was no one else in the room to ask, I figured it was okay to help myself.

Well of course I got caught. My mom came in just as I was licking the remaining dreamy whoopie pie filling off the plastic wrapper on the floor. When she asked me if I ate it I gave her my most innocent look, as if to say, "Whoopie pie? I thought you said "*woofie* pie!" But she wasn't buying it. She knew I had rationalized my actions and that I knew what I did was wrong.

There's a duality to everything in life. Death makes life sweet. The dawn contrasts against the night. The calm happens before and after the storm. Just like it says in the Bible, to everything there is a season; however, there are certain dualities that cannot coexist: Faith and fear; tolerance and ignorance; love and hate. And as I barked earlier, there's a fine line between being so accommodating that you actually rationalize away what you stand for.

A double-minded person is one who says one thing and does another; they claim to believe one thing yet their actions do not live up to such claims. They often speak with a forked tongue, saying things that are either blatant lies or delivering promises that they have no intention of keeping. They think about two different things at the same time and can't make up their minds about anything; they are dually focused and have split opinions. As they say in the good book, they are unstable in everything they do. So, Saucy Aussie, pick one course of action, one purpose, one pack, and live like you mean it. As Matthew 6:24 says, "No one can serve two masters. Either you will hate the one and love the other, or you will be devoted to the one and despise the other. You cannot serve both God and money." In dog lingo, if you chase two rabbits, they will both get away.

In a previous chapter, we talked about how critical it is that whatever you say you *are*, you live your life authentically. Your public and your private dogmas must be in sync. My mom once had a boss who was extremely dogmatic in certain work situations, while being the kindest, gentlest pup she'd ever seen in others. This made it extremely difficult to know if he was going to bear his fangs or wag his tail, and my mom did her best to steer clear of him.

Saucy Aussies do not chase two rabbits. They decide what they are focused on and committed to, and they do everything they can to acquire it. And if you've ever seen an Australian shepherd at work, you know the intense focus I'm talking about. Sure, different rabbits may come in and out of your life throughout the years, but just make sure that what you're chasing is compatible with your three major decisions in life; otherwise, everything and everyone else may get away.

"When a decision has to be made, make it. There is no totally right time for anything."
—General George S. Patton

Atten-hut!

Four-Star Leadership for Leaders: Interviews with
Distinguished Generals and Admirals
by R. Manning Ancell

I just love hearing my mom's stories about when she was in the Air Force. I gather from what she's said that humans do not get to achieve this level of rank in the pack unless they are willing to make the ultimate sacrifice for their convictions and is certain of which side of the fence they are on. After all, their decisions mean the difference between life and death, victory and defeat. Their actions determine the fates of nations and place an indelible stamp upon history. They are four-star generals and admirals, our country's top-ranking military leadership, and in *Four-Star Leadership for Leaders*, they offer their hard-won expertise to you.

Military leaders are a unique breed. They have taken an oath of allegiance to preserve and defend the Constitution of the United States against all enemies, foreign and domestic. Any dereliction of duty or rationalization of results could prove disastrous. Author R. Manning Ancell spent nearly forty years interviewing the very highest echelon of our armed forces. This book is transcribed from personal, in-depth interviews with each one of them as they shared their views on leadership, delegation, developing people, and handling adversity.

From the First World War to the Second Gulf War, these are the leaders who showed the way under the most challenging circumstances imaginable. Let their words guide you through the battlefields of business and life and show you which side of the fence you need to be on!

The Ruby Red Family Gallery

Jane Pawsten

Jane Pawsten, who lived in England, was one of the first writers in our family. Her works, which included *Dog-sense and Dog-sensibility* and *Pride and Paw-judice*, highlighted the roles of lady-dogs in Regency-era England. She earned her place as one of the most widely-read writers in doggie literature.

Amelia Barkhart

Some doggies walk. Some run. Some even jump. This one flew! Amelia Barkhart was the first lady-dog to fly across both the Atlantic and Pacific Oceans. She was even awarded the Distinguished Flying Cross by Congress in 1932!

Doggie Barkton

Born the fourth of twelve in Tennessee, Ms. Barkton was always ashamed of her two biggest attributes: her ears. Because of them, though, she found that she could hear music very well—and sing even better! She became a world-renowned singer, actress, and member of the Country Music Hall of Fame.

Eleanor Roofsevelt

Although she was very shy when she was but a pup, Ms. Roofsevelt came into her own when she took her place in the role of First Lady-Dog. She was very out-barken and championed many noble causes, including human rights, women's issues, and children's causes.

"Queenie" Esther

We know about "Queenie" Esther from the Old Testament "Book of Esther." She was a young pup living in exile and then became queen of an entire empire! She saved may of her kind from destruction through her courage and humility.

Joan of Barc

From the French side of our family comes Joan of Barc. She became a hero after fighting against and repulsing the English from her country during the Hundred Years' War. While she was a great and courageous fighter, she was not a good cook, as she was known to burn her steaks.

Maggie "The Iron Doggie" Thatcher

Because she was so tough, our Aunt Maggie earned the name "The Iron Doggie." She was the first lady-dog Prime Minister of the United Kingdom. She led England out of a recession, defended the Falkland Islands, and stood her ground against the Soviet Union. She coined the phrase "Talk to the paw!"

Mary Kay Akbash

While some doggies scratch for fleas, Mary Kay Akbash built a business from scratch! With a small investment and lots of hind-paw grease, Mary Kay built a cosmetics empire. Her profitable business creates new opportunities for lady-dogs to achieve financial success.

"Mommie" Teresa

A great lady-doggie, our "Mommie" Teresa devoted her life to working amongst the poorest of the poor and the strayest of the strays. No doggie was ever left hungry or without proper care under her watchful and tender eyes.

Rosa Barks

A lady-dog of great courage, Rosa Barks was not one to be pushed around. Her refusal to surrender her seat on a bus spurred the 381-day city-wide Montgomery Bus Boycott, making it one of the most successful mass movements against segregation in history.

Sacapawea

Back when the United States was still being settled,
Sacapawea went with Lewis and Clark on their
expedition. Even though she had a puppy at the time,
she helped in many ways as a skilled translator. To this
day, she is honored with statues, stamps, and coins.

Tina Terrier

After suffering years of abuse from her husband and performance partner Spike, Tina Terrier established herself as a successful solo barker and performer. She became world famous and epitomizes the ability to get a second leash and write a happy ending.

Let Sleeping Dogs Lie

6

To Err Is Human; To Forgive, Canine

According to the *Encarta World English Dictionary*, a grudge match is defined as "a match between players or teams who have a long-standing animosity between them or a specific past insult or injury to revenge." The whole point of this book is to teach you humans some tips about how to take hurt, which by the way is universal to all living things, and use it to make you *better* and not *bitter*. Grudges make you bitter. They harden you over the years and make your heart go cold. They kill a bit of your soul every moment that you hold on to them. Malachy McCourt said it best, "Holding a grudge is like drinking poison and then hoping that the other person dies."

We've all heard the phrase "let sleeping dogs lie." Although the Old Testament book of Proverbs makes references to the foolish mishandling of dogs, many sources point to the English author Geoffrey Chaucer as the originator of the idiom. Other authors have since used variations on Chaucer's theme to imply the inherent dangers of awakening sleeping dogs.

45

The modern form of the idiom is more passive in nature, suggesting that sleeping dogs, especially large and volatile breeds, should remain undisturbed. In Chaucer's time, the proverb warned against deliberately approaching a sleeping dog and forcefully awakening it. Anyone who chooses to wake up a sleeping guard dog generally gets the punishment he deserves.

Why on earth do humans insist on popping poisonous pills called "grudges"? Why do they stir up old conflicts, open old wounds, or start fights over past issues? Let bygones be bygones. Whether they've been resolved or unresolved, it is best to "agree to disagree" and move forward rather than opening up an old wound or hot spot that will only ensure the start of much snarling and snapping. Some hounds instinctively lash out when someone awakens them unexpectedly from a deep sleep, much like you humans do! It's a natural response to something unexpected or unwelcome.

My brother, Mr. Blue, has a hot spot on his back-right paw that he's been messing with for years. Just after it gets healed up he starts licking or chewing at it again. He really has to fight the urge to pick at it. Many people have hot spots in their relationships or jobs. Maybe it's a fight over an unpaid bill, or cross words exchanged years ago. This little spot can bring back previous memories of arguments from the past and escalate the current discussion into a snarling match!

It's best not to dredge up the past. When you do, that's called "hitting below the belt." And it's a dirty technique. Not good dirty, like rolling around on dead or stinky things, but bad dirty, like totally un-Saucy Aussie behavior. Bringing up past negative experiences never helps resolve the current situ-

> "If you continuously chase your tail, you'll never get away from the stink."
> —Mr. Blue

ation, so let that sleeping dog lie and keep your yapper shut! As my *grandpaw*, Charlie "Tremendous" Jones, said, "No one is a failure until they blame somebody else." So let's stay away from our urge to rewrite history and leave the past in the past.

Unresolved grudges or long-standing feuds in the business world or your personal life can dramatically benefit from this stance. A project manager may have had an unpleasant working relationship with a subordinate in the past, but a new project requires complete team cooperation. Rather than sabotage group unity, the project manager and his coworker may agree to let sleeping dogs lie where their personal disagreements are concerned. Maybe you and a close friend had a falling out years ago. If these past issues are largely resolved and have little bearing on the present situation, then it is better for everyone that they remain dormant. As the saying goes, "Time heals all wounds." My mom had a decorative plate that read, "I don't repeat gossip, so listen close the first time." While this is worthy of a chuckle, it really is best to let much of our non-edifying conversational points remain unsaid. When in doubt, resist the urge to bark it out.

Did you know there is a verse in Proverbs, Chapter 26, that says, "Like a dog that returns to his vomit is a fool who repeats his folly"? OK, take it easy! Don't shout out "Gross" so loud. People will wonder what's up! Now we hounds are certainly just about the most perfect species in the animal kingdom, but we do have this one trait that is beyond the comprehension of our humans. We acknowledge it, it's no secret, and you love us regardless, which is why I even dared to bring it up! But the point is well-made with this analogy. If it's unsavory of man's best friend to return

"He who angers you conquers you."
—Elizabeth Kenny

to his vomit, why do you humans repeat the same repulsive act by continuing your folly? Let it be!

Today's world of reality television takes great pleasure in exploiting humans by encouraging their tendencies to stir each other up and take bites out of one another. It is so sad and disturbing for us canines to watch our beloved humans act in such a manner. After all, you're the ones who domesticated us to be the most obedient and loyal creatures on Earth! Being civil in disagreement and discourse is no longer applauded or publicized. But that's where the Saucy Aussie is different. We have actually risen above the lowly desire of some people to operate on a dog-eat-dog level and can tell them to "Talk to the paw!"

Don't repeat past mistakes, don't fantasize about ways to take revenge, don't keep bringing up old transgressions, don't open old wounds, let bygones be bygones, do *not* make a mountain out of a molehill, and don't return to your own folly. When you engage in this type of behavior, you've become a vomit eater! And I'm pretty sure you humans do *not* get the same enjoyment out of it that we hounds do.

The Only Thing We Have to Fear...

Freedom From Fear

by Mark Matteson

Ever since reading Hannah Hurnard's *Hinds' Feet on High Places* when she was a young pup, my mom has been a big fan of parables. *Freedom From Fear* is the story about a rush-hour fender bender on a sweltering summer day, which turns out to be the experience of a lifetime.

When Steve, depressed and miserable, literally runs into Len on an especially bad day, the stage is set for a life-changing experience of the first magnitude. Steve has unwittingly placed himself in the hands of a master motivator and attitude adjuster. As Steve begins to improve his outlook (and his life!), he starts to see the ways in which Len has touched the lives of countless others. He teaches Steve to let go of the past and in doing so to break free from the bondage of fear. Life is too short to be saddled with so many of the grudges we drag from decade to decade.

Len waits in these pages, and he has a message for you too. This book is chock-full of lessons, bullet points, and places at the end of each chapter for you to write your own thoughts. Read *Freedom From Fear* and let Len's wisdom unleash the Saucy Aussie in you!

"Holding on to anger is like grasping a hot coal with the intent of throwing it at someone else; you are the one who gets burned."

—Buddha

You Don't Have to Be the Lead Dog...

7

...To Have an Amazing View

I'm a purebred Australian shepherd, so my genetic coding is a little different from my multicultural siblings who are magnificent mutts. I am a clear reflection of everything that defines the temperament and appearance of my breed. I am more vocal and outgoing, while my two blue merle Aussie mix brothers are much more mellow and laid back. We used to all go out for walks together, but my mom got tired of having to go to the chiropractor from us pulling her arms and legs in fifteen different directions every day.

Now, she takes me for a walk separate from my two brothers. This works out great because their stride is very different from mine. Due to their mix of doggie DNA (basset hound and corgi), they have much shorter legs and always have their noses to the ground examining every single inch of the walk. I guess when you're that close to the ground you have a very different perspective. It's step-sniff-mark or step-sniff-taste every single inch of the way! They are quite tactical in their approach with their heads down and noses to the grindstone enjoying every single detail and nuance.

I'm the opposite. I have long legs for an Aussie and my head is always up and moving from side to side, scanning the horizon for what we might encounter. Is it a squirrel? A leaf blowing in the distance? Another four-legger? Some children I can kiss on the face? I am more strategic in my view. I revel in looking far off into the distance and seeing the big picture. It's what I'm good at, so you are best to keep me on a loose leash at a brisk pace with plenty of scenery to scan. My brothers are the exact opposite!

Do my brothers and I both have phenomenal times with my mom on our separate walks even though our views are completely different? Yes we do! I may not fully grasp why my siblings are so busy leaving Post-it notes everywhere and dragging their noses on the ground, but it's what they enjoy doing. So sniff and let sniff, I say! You do your thing and I'll do mine.

Humans have a dog colloquialism: "Unless you're the lead dog, the scenery never changes." I guess people take this to mean that if you aren't the leader of the pack, the only thing you get to look at all day long is other butts. And while we dogs are pack animals, not all of us grab each other by the throats to be the top dog like some bad humans do. In our pack, somebody steps up to take the lead position and we all fall into our places accordingly. In fact, many of us are quite happy to assume a more submissive or secondary role. It isn't any less important or less of a view and, most importantly, it's just a better fit for some dogs. And a happy dog is a dog that gets to display its true temperament and genetic coding.

Some humans think that because they are the top dogs they can look down on everyone else. Never look down on someone unless it is to extend to him an uplifting paw. As Ralph Waldo Emerson said, "A great man is always willing to be little." When my mom was in the Air Force, she assumed that everyone wanted to get promoted to be a chief or a four-star general. But she found out that some different people have different desires and are perfectly happy and actualized with the ranks they achieved.

Some loved being crew chiefs and wanted to launch jets for twenty years. Some of the engineers and scientists she worked with wanted nothing more than to be an individual contributor and create designs by dissecting drawings and creating patents day after day. Still others had the 30,000-foot view and excelled at more "big-picture" projects, defining creative long-term solutions or plans. As long as you are fully utilizing your own strengths and unique gifts, every view is different and every view is tremendous!

You are the lead dog in your ring of life! You determine the best position for yourself where you can do what you want to do. You determine your own path or whom you want to follow. Do you want to strike out on life's incredible journey on your own, foraging through with your individual might and wits? Or do you want to follow someone else's scent and be a part of a larger pack. It's all good, as long as you are enjoying life's walk each step of the way.

You are not obligated to succeed. You are only obligated to do your best. And if you must judge people, make sure it's from where they stand, not from where you stand. My *grandpaw*, Charlie "Tremendous" Jones, said it best: "One of life's great challenges is to quit acting and start being." Whatever your view is,

"If you judge people, you have no time to love them."
—Mother Teresa of Calcutta

> **"A man sooner or later discovers that he is the master-gardener of his soul, the director of his life."**
> —James Allen

claim it, own it, and live by it. Find your spot and enjoy it! Don't be a wayward pup running from pack to pack, chasing this tail and then that one. Stand firm and guard your bone, pack, or domicile.

A group of construction workers sat down to eat lunch together daily. One of the workers would open his lunch box every day and exclaim, "*Oh no!* Not peanut butter sandwiches!" After several days of this same behavior his buddy finally asked him, "Joe, take it easy. Why don't you just tell your wife not to pack any more peanut butter sandwiches?" "You leave my wife out of this," Joe exclaimed. "I pack my own lunch!"

A Saucy Aussie knows that the view is most exquisite when you are doing exactly what you are meant to do; when your individual personality or breed, your specific gifts and talents, and your chosen work are all in sync. You'll never tire of looking at it, even when the going gets ruff or you've bitten off more peanut butter and jelly sandwiches than you can chew. It's where you were meant to be and you're doing what you were born to do.

A Saucy Aussie knows that if you find your true place in the pack of life, you'll never get tired of the view!

A Book by My Grandpaw

The Price of Leadership

by Charlie "Tremendous" Jones

My mom told me she heard my *grandpaw* deliver *The Price of Leadership* speech hundreds of times. As a young pup, she said she remembered listening in wonderment at the price required to be a leader. Every worthwhile view has a price, and leadership is no different. After all, we are leading all the time.

It wasn't until my mom's professional years that she began to glimpse the price you must pay in order to enjoy your place in the pack. Growing up, her father showed her through his life that it required loneliness, weariness, abandonment, and vision. It's only when you are willing and begin to take the action required that you understand the price of leadership and are comfortable in your own fur.

This speech originated when my *grandpaw* was fresh from the trenches of the life insurance industry. He loved this industry and it produced some of the greatest salespeople ever. His stories reflect the activities and responses of a young salesman passionate about sharing the security he found in the industry with others. It also includes a very pragmatic and humorous assessment of things that come out of employees' and prospects' mouths and how to stay motivated regardless.

The greatest takeaway from this little speech is that the next time you sit in your office alone, with your forehead in your hands, abandoned by the very ones you're trying so hard to assist, so **"Everybody is a genius. But if you judge a fish by its ability to climb a tree, it will live its whole life believing that it is stupid."**
—Albert Einstein

tired you don't think you can go on, and you're the only one who seems to grasp the vision of what needs to be done, know that you are truly on the road to learning what it takes to pay the price of leadership. And know that you are learning to really live!

This little gem will teach every Saucy Aussie what they can expect before they can enjoy the most tremendous view imaginable!

Every Dog Has Its Day

8

How K-9 Karma Opened the Doggie Door of Opportunity

There I was in my breeding cage, unable to climb to a higher level, locked up and knocked up. I had no idea the proverbial "lid" could be lifted and my current existence could change. But hear this, humans and hounds: **Despite every let-down, smackdown, shutdown, and put-down you've ever endured, you will have your day.** It may not be right when you want it, but it will happen. We canines have karma too. That's where the saying came from: "Every dog has its day," At least that's what I heard around the kennel. That's why all those people who take such wonderful care of us have a ton of good stuff coming their way and those who haven't will have it *ruff*! Woof!

You say, "Ms. Ruby, life's not fair! I haven't done any bad stuff to anyone, but all this hurt has been done to me! When will I have my day?"

Talk to the paw! That's right my friend, life is not fair and no reliable source ever claimed it would be. Oscar Wilde even

57

said, "Life is never fair, and perhaps it is a good thing for most of us that it is not." The only thing I'd ever done in my life was to be born to someone who only saw me as a breeding animal and a source of income! Bad things happen to good humans and hounds, no doubt about it. But thankfully life is not about what happens to you, but how you respond to what happens to you.

My *grandpaw*, Charlie "Tremendous" Jones, said, "Things don't go wrong and break your heart so you can become bitter and give up. They happen to break you down and build you up so you can be all that you were intended to be." Boy, if that doesn't put your past and present circumstances on the path to a more tremendous future, I don't know what will!

Everyone has doggie doo-doo done to them. The bad news is it's an embedded part of your human nature. It's even called the human condition. The good news is that it can motivate you to overcome adversity and become all you were meant to be. "@#it" rolls downhill, so sometime, somewhere, you're going to get hit with a ton of it. But that doesn't mean you have to wallow in it. Get up and move! If you're up to your elbows in alligators, you have an opportunity to get out of it. As Albert Einstein said, "In the midst of adversity is opportunity." So move!

You say, "Wait, I have no opportunities where I am." Talk to the paw! Keep looking, keep on watching, and keep on sniffing out a plan. It will happen, so you've got to be ready to *springer* into action because things can change at a moment's notice. Always remember: You make your own opportunities. As my *grand-*

> **"Let Hercules himself do what he may. The cat will mew and dog will have his day."**
> **—William Shakespeare**

paw said, "Success is based more on availability than ability." Sooner or **"There is not security on this earth. There is only opportunity."**
—Gen. Douglas MacArthur

later you will find the courage or assistance to free yourself from emotional, physical, or financial bondage. You humans are much more able to change your circumstances than we hounds are. You have opposable thumbs that can get you out of and away from many of the bad things that we can't. You can open doors and locks and move out of bad situations; so quit complaining and get moving!

My *grandpaw* only made it through the eighth grade, yet he was known as one of the wisest people and speakers of his time. His family pack got separated several times when he was a young pup. He didn't have a shiny coat or nice clothes to wear. He grew up in a pup tent, not a nice home. But this lack of pedigree only made him work harder! Since he was not born into anything, he took nothing for granted and made the most out of every opportunity that came his way. He had a hungry mind that he fed through a habit of voracious reading. Reading great books showed him that there was an infinite amount of doggie doors he could open. And because he knew rejection as a youth, just like many of us, he made it his life's mission to make everyone feel special. His friend, Jim Rohn, once said, "Formal education will make you a living; self-education will make you a fortune." Can we all work harder to educate ourselves? Why yes, we can! The key is to have an attitude of self-worth and purpose. If we don't do it for ourselves, nobody will. You can be a leader because leaders are made, not born.

Everyone has the same amount of opportunities; it's the circumstances that are different. You can achieve your dreams

"Every dog has his day, unless he loses his tail, then he has a weak-end."
—June Carter

if you work toward them. It's the results that are personalized. Just as every dog has his day, every man has his place in the world. While you are busy growling about all the closed doors of opportunity, you forget that you've got to get off your haunches and bolt through the doggie door of destiny before you can experience what's on the other side! Napoleon Hill, one of the greatest thinkers in the history of man, said, "Opportunity often comes in the form of misfortune or temporary defeat." So in actuality, the more downtrodden you are, the greater your opportunities. Woof! This means that failure is psychological, and that it is within your power and ability to ornament your second leash on life to reflect exactly what it is you want.

If a bad boss puts you down, saying "that dog don't hunt," show him he's wrong. Find a career field where you can charge up and down the hillside freely, putting all your God-given talents to use! If someone who's been using you tells you they no longer need you, rejoice! Anyone that selfish you most definitely want to run as far away from as possible. It was so scary being dumped at the pound, and I almost blew it by being aggressive with everyone and every dog there! But in the end I calmed down enough to have my day just long enough for someone to give me a second leash on life.

Want to have your day? What's stopping you? Nothing, other than what's in your mind. It's all up to you to work at it until you get it! As Jeremy Collier said, "Everyone has a fair turn to be as great as he pleases." So take hold of your own leash and walk yourself right through that doggie door of opportunity, you Saucy Aussie, and make your day today!

The Epitome of Getting a Second Leash

Advantages of Poverty
by Andrew Carnegie

Advantages of Poverty is a dynamic book that encapsulates the life and wisdom of the millionaire philanthropist and "steel king," Andrew Carnegie, with brief biographical information along with portions of his essays. This book epitomizes the essence of getting a second leash on life. You will read about a man who came from intense poverty yet went on the make more millionaires than anyone else. He went to only four years of school, yet wrote eight books and donated millions of dollars toward the advancement of education.

You will discover the attitude of selfless giving that motivated this innovative businessman who helped various communities, charities, and organizations to achieve greater success during his day. Andrew Carnegie had his day and helped countless other have theirs too. His goal was to establish free libraries so that poor pups could be just as well-read as the ones from wealthy packs.

The wisdom of the steel tycoon who emigrated from Scotland will undoubtedly inspire you to recognize the advantages of an exceptional work ethic that overcomes poverty and lack of birthright, and that you, too, will have your day. I worked hard to get my second leash on life, and now I have the most tremendous *furever* home in the world! As the author himself said, "I have had to deal with great sums. Many millions of dollars have since passed through my hands. But the genuine satisfaction I had from that one dollar

"It takes courage to grow up and turn out to be who you really are."
—e.e. cummings

and twenty cents outweighs any subsequent pleasure in money-getting. It was the direct reward of honest, manual labor."

Andrew Carnegie epitomized the life purpose of administering everything you have to the betterment of others before you die. He declared it was a "disgrace to die rich," and in embodying this credo, he helped countless Saucy Aussies "have their day" because his hard work and generosity with his resources gave them a second leash on life.

"Courage is being scared to death but saddling up anyway."
—John Wayne

The Flea-Dip Principle

9

Cleanliness Is Next to Dog-liness

Admit it, most of you do not think about dogs when you think about cleanliness. Talk to the paw! You humans have fleas too! I'm barking about the parasites that infest all of our lives with their life-sucking negativity. My *grandpaw*, Charlie "Tremendous" Jones, said "You'll be the same person you are today five years from now except for two things; the people you meet and the books you read. If you want to be a better leader, hang out with better leaders; if you want to be a better parent, hang out with better parents; if you want to be a better whining, thumb-sucking bonehead, hang out with better whining, thumb-sucking boneheads."

If you are hanging out with fleabags, guess what? You're a fleabag! But if you want to be a top dog, hang out with other top dogs. It's that simple. Just like the saying "Birds of a feather flock together,"

"Success is failure with the dirt brushed off."
—Mamie McCullough

remember: "Mongrels in a pack will attack." So be careful with whom you're spending time because a little bit of them always rubs off or jumps

"He that lieth down with dogs shall rise up with fleas."
—Benjamin Franklin

onto you. It's called guilt by association, and the bad scent of a dirty deed or a dalliance can linger on long after you part ways. So watch out!

I used to take offense at Mr. Franklin's flea quote. I mean, how rude! My momma may wear combat boots but she most definitely doesn't have fleas! However, now I understand that the focus isn't on the dog, but on the *fleas*. Fleas are small, leaping, blood-sucking insects—parasites that live off of warm-blooded animals. Gross! Once they've set up house, they are extremely difficult to get rid of. And if you do manage to get rid of them, just letting one of these vermin back in will infect your entire world! My backside is getting itchy just thinking about them!

As a dog, I can tell you that I cannot have some areas of my *furever* home flea-free and the others infected. The same is true for your work and home environment. You can't run a successful organization when you have some managers who keep their environment flea-free and others who don't. Fleas don't honor organizational charts and chains of command. They jump freely from one group to the next, infecting as many as they can. It only takes one; they multiply faster than rabbits and get on absolutely everyone.

So what is a flea in a professional sense? It can take many forms. It can manifest itself in the form of workers who display laziness, bad attitudes, and negative actions. It manifests itself in corporate scenarios as supervisors who don't want to enforce standards, disengaged or hostile workers, and management or employee bashers.

You can have your own personal fleas as well. While you may have your financial house in order, your health may be horrible due to some habits you will not break. You may maintain a strict code of business ethics but do not honor your personal vows to your family. You may be responsible for making thousands of command decisions each day, yet not be able to discipline your own children. You have to maintain discipline in all areas of your life. You'll never be as effective as you can be until you fumigate your entire life and surround yourself with other top dogs who hate fleas in all areas of their lives as much as you do.

When I was first evaluated, the Dog Whisperer had a complete list of all the things that might trigger aggression in me. Food, other dogs, children, strangers, separation, the leash, cars, bicycles; the list went on and on. About half of these trigger chiggers got under my fur. Did my mom stop training me after I got rid of just one of them? No! What kind of a Saucy Aussie would I be if I learned to accept cars and other dogs, but snapped at children? I needed a complete overhaul of all the negative response triggers in my life until they were totally fumigated. And I require constant reinforcement in the form of praise, recognition and rewards, so they don't enter my doggone noggin' again.

Getting a clean environment starts with a complete housecleaning. You can take a dog and put him in a flea dip to get rid of the fleas, but if you put him back in the same environment, he's going to get fleas again. That's why it's imperative to have leaders

> "People often say that motivation doesn't last. Well, neither does bathing—that's why we recommend it daily."
> —Zig Ziglar

who support accountability across the board and insist on it at the individual level. All it takes is one flea-bitten, paw-sucking manager to let the fleas creep back in and re-infest

"Let a single flea stay on thee and soon you'll be in misery."
—**Ruby Red**

your entire organization! Do not associate with negative or lazy people who will be a parasitic drain on you. Implement a plan to break free of unhealthy habits in your life. And for people who say, "Hey, when it gets to something important, I'll step up and do the right thing," I say, "Talk to the paw!" One of my mom's all-time favorite quotes about this very principle is by Gen. George S. Patton: "If you can't get them to salute when they should salute and wear the clothes you tell them to wear, how are you going to get them to die for their country?" If you can't deal with fleas, you'll never be able to handle the much larger parasites and bloodsuckers out there.

So for all you Saucy Aussies in the making out there, it's time to honestly answer the question, "Is my environment flea-free or do I need to schedule a fumigation?" Cleanliness is next to *dog-liness*. We dogs love a clean doggie bed to plop down on and an environment free from parasites. So do humans. But we have to work like dogs to ensure these little varmints stay off our property! It's an all-or-nothing proposition that takes work every day of the year. As Mr. Ziglar so eloquently put it, "They say motivation doesn't last, neither does bathing. That's why we recommend it daily." Think these bloodsuckers are too embedded in your life and organization to ban them for good? Talk to the paw! It's never too late to fumigate.

"Change the changeable, accept the unchangeable, and remove yourself from the unacceptable."
—**Denis Waitley**

I Double-Dog Dare You!

I Dare You!
by William H. Danforth

This is one of the all-time motivational classics written by the founder of the Ralston Purina Company in Saint Louis, Missouri, so he must know what he's talking about! Woof! But that's not the only reason every Saucy Aussie needs to read this book.

My mom said she remembers first reading *I Dare You!* when she was ten years old. She was intrigued about being "dared" and wanted to implement all the ideas in this book so that she could courageously take on all the opportunities and challenges that life had to offer.

Mr. Danforth's book presents life as a checkerboard. All four aspects—mental, physical, social, and religious—must be sufficiently nurtured to maximize your success. It is a sound philosophy that many great organizations have come to embrace, and my mom remembers it being taught at the Air Force Academy. A successful life is a balanced life.

Saucy Aussies know that all areas of their lives must be continuously cleansed in order to banish vermin such as negative thoughts and bad habits. We are in a constant state of housekeeping, and reading a book like this gives you a wealth of tools for your heart, mind, and soul that'll make you worthy of winning best in show!

"The word 'politics' is of Latin origin: 'Poli' means many and 'tics' means blood suckers!"
—Charlie "Tremendous" Jones

Man's Best Friends Are Dog-Eared

10

The Best Things in Life Are Free to a Good Home

Icopied this last chapter from my older brother, Mr. Blue. It's just so tasty that I had to include it in my masterpiece; plus, Mr. Blue is the wisest hound I know. He was exposed to *pawsitive* reading material at five weeks of age and was raised in an atmosphere of encouragement. It took me until I was six years old before I heard my first words of motivation instead of someone barking orders at me. But just to let you know, these eternal truths are satisfying and enlightening no matter how far you are in life's journey. So get off your haunches and run to the nearest bookstore or library! Sometimes I think they mean more to me than they do to my brother because I can see how far I've come.

Man's best friend, it has been said, is a dog. While my mom would most certain-

"Outside of a dog, a book is man's best friend. Inside of a dog it's too dark to read."
—Groucho Marx

"Books are the quietest and most constant of friends; they are the most accessible and wisest of counselors, and the most patient of teachers."
—Charles W. Eliot

ly agree with this, and I would echo that sentiment, there is another loyal, unconditionally loving, joy-bringing, by-your-bed-at-night friend that we have repeatedly talked about: a book!

While I will cross over the Rainbow Bridge one day, books have the essence of immortality *now*. They will live until the end of time. They can speak to you in a way that your spouse, boss, friend, or even a pet cannot. They find words when you are unable and become your voice when you cannot speak. And while I have certainly transformed my mom's life as she has mine, the power of a book to illuminate the past, create a present, and unveil the future is unparalleled and well-documented. Books can be one of the greatest catalysts in helping a Saucy Aussie get a second leash on life!

They say every dog has its day and that alone makes it worth reading about! I can read about Guinefort, the Saint of Infants, who was a French greyhound who protected his master's infant from attack by a snake. Stubby, a decorated canine veteran of World War I, achieved the rank of sergeant, actually captured a German spy, and courageously fought in seventeen battles. Woof! Laika, the courageous Soviet high-altitude flight and space dog, was an integral part of her country's space program. Dogs discovered the West with Lewis and Clark and even saved the life of Napoleon Bonaparte when he fell overboard.

My mom gets hundreds of e-mails from people telling her about a particular book my *grandpaw* had sniffed out and given to them that had changed their lives! Imagine that; you give someone the gift of a book and it changes their life! What other gift can you give someone that has that type of power? Talk about a *pawsome* return on investment. Books are the perfect counselor and confidant. They don't judge or presume. You get to take exactly what you need from the words on the page when you need them the most. What other treasure can say that? The paw, I mean *hand*, that picks up a book is never the same one that puts it down.

You know what they say: Book lovers never sleep alone! And that goes double for those who love dogs (triple if you love and own cats too!). And although dogs do exhibit a high degree of unconditional love, it's books that truly remain steadfast under all circumstances, even when you stack them on a shelf or leave them in moving boxes in the basement or attic and forget about them for decades. They are always there and ready whenever you are.

For those of you not familiar with the English colloquialism "hair of the dog," it refers to a treatment aimed at lessening the effects of a hangover after a night of debauchery. Its origins came from the treatment of a rabid dog bite where hair from the dog was placed in the wound. Books are the ultimate hair of the dog. They cure all the headaches, fatigue, and pains of the previous day, especially if you've bitten off more than you can chew. A few words purposefully read and inserted into your heart, mind, or soul can suck the poison out of any wound. Remember, if you can carry it in your hand, you can carry it in your heart.

"One can find or make no better friend than a good book."

—J.C. Penney

The greatest commonality between books and dogs is their ears. My mom loves to dog-ear the pages of a book when she finds great quotes or thoughts that have impacted her. In fact, I think if you looked at the books we've read, every other page would be dog-eared! And she loves to massage my dog ears at night as I drift off to sleep and let out that final sigh. Sometimes there are tears of love, joy, or revelation on both of our dog ears, which makes me feel extremely close to my mom. In each case, dog ears signify something pretty tremendous!!

The wisdom of a book and the loyalty of a dog: The best things in life really are free!

"Books have meant to my life what the sun has meant to the planet Earth."
—Earl Nightingale

My Grandpaw Is Pawsome!

Books Are Tremendous

edited by Charlie "Tremendous" Jones

Think now that you've graduated from puppy preschool you know it all? Think again. All Saucy Aussies are continuous readers. If you are large and in charge but haven't pawed through a single transformational book in the last month, may I suggest you take a long, deep drink from the water bowl of reality.

This little gem will put you on the scent for great books. It's chock-full of quotes and excerpts from some of the greatest minds of all time talking about the power of reading and the source of power found in a book. "Been there, done that" is the credo of mediocrity for those content to rest on their haunches. According to my *grandpaw*, here's why you should read:

Don't read to be smart; read to be real.

Don't read to be big; read to be down to earth.

Don't read to memorize; read to realize.

Don't read to learn; read to unlearn what you never should have learned in the first place.

And don't read a lot; read just enough to get your mind stimulated and thinking, and to get you curious and hungry to keep you learning all your life!

Want to be as loyal, trustworthy, hard working, and genuine as a dog? Then read, doggone it! Books are our leashes to everything that ever was and everything that can be! Readers are not only leaders, they are believers! Reading helps you see things in a different light and can enhance your entire belief system. Read books that most resemble really meaty bones; ones that give you a lot to chew on and savor for hours and even days. Read books that make you dig way down deep inside, like a miner digging for gold or me digging for my bone!

"A man's reading program
should be as carefully planned
as his daily diet, for that too
is food, without which he
cannot grow mentally."
—Andrew Carnegie

How are you going to begin grabbing for that second leash?

Use this space for notes about how you are going to grab that second leash and become better and not bitter...

Two Great Books from...

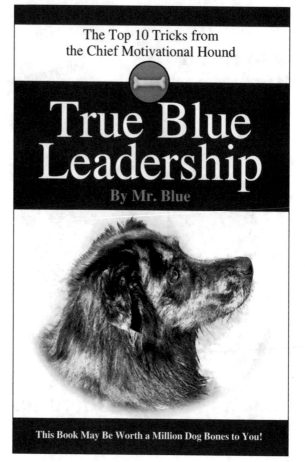

The Top 10 Tricks from
the Chief Motivational Hound

True Blue Leadership
By Mr. Blue

This Book May Be Worth a Million Dog Bones to You!

Everyone knows that dogs have it all figured out, so why not learn to lead from man's best friend? The granddog of Charlie "Tremendous" Jones, Mr. Blue learned at the feet of the masters, gathering a great storehouse of wisdom from legendary speakers and authors, all of which he shares in *True Blue Leadership: Top 10 Tricks From the Chief Motivational Hound*.

Available wherever fine books are sold or at
www.TremendousLifeBooks.com.

...Ruby Red's Brother, Mr. Blue!

The full-color children's companion to *True Blue Leadership: Top 10 Tricks from the Chief Motivational Hound*!

What's the Difference Between a Wonderdog and an Underdog? A Wonderdog Gets Bones...and an Underdog Gets Fleas!

It can be tough growing up. I should know! I used to be a pup just like you and boy did I have it ruff. I was lucky, though, because I had some great teachers (like my *grandpaw* Charlie "Tremendous" Jones) who taught me a lot of really *pawsome* things that kept me out of the doghouse and made me the *pawsitive* Wonderdog that I am today.

I'm *furever barkful* that I got the chance to learn those wonderful lessons—and that's why I want to share them with you.

Available wherever fine books are sold or at
www.TremendousLifeBooks.com.

About the Pawthor

Ruby Red

Ruby Red is a seven-year-old Australian Shepherd who currently enjoys the position of Chief Excitement Officer at Tremendous Life Books. When not performing her duties at work or *pawthoring* books, Ruby Red is an avid butt-wiggler and vocal contortionist, loves mothering all small animals and children, and is prone to bouts of spontaneous affection.

Tracey C. Jones

Other than being Ruby Red's human mom and translator, Tracey C. Jones is the president of Tremendous Life Books. Her father, the late Charlie "Tremendous" Jones, started Executive Books for the purpose of changing the world one book at a time. With an exceptional leadership background, Tracey became the company's new president in 2009 and continues to carry on her father's legacy.